A Mind of a Broken Heart

ONE FAMILY'S JOURNEY

Tammy Glamp-Siligrini

TRILOGY CHRISTIAN PUBLISHERS
TUSTIN, CA

Trilogy Christian Publishers
A Wholly Owned Subsidiary of Trinity Broadcasting Network
2442 Michelle Drive
Tustin, CA 92780

For information about special discounts for bulk purchases, please contact Trilogy Christian Publishing.

Manufactured in the United States of America

10 9 8 7 6 5 4 3 2 1

Library of Congress Cataloging-in-Publication Data is available.

ISBN 978-1-64773-766-5

ISBN 978-1-64773-767-2 (ebook)

Contents

Dedication

This book is dedicated to all the men and women who have struggled in their addictions and stubborn habits. And to those who do truly suffer from bipolar disorder. I personally want to encourage you that true freedom is Jesus Christ. He shed his blood on Calvary for you over 2000 years ago. On that cross, he was thinking of you. He was, and still is, concerned with your cares, your fears, and your desires. "But seek ye first the kingdom of God and his righteousness; and all these things shall be added unto you" (Matthew 6:33, KJV).

To my children, James Glamp, Robert Glamp, Joseph Siligrini, Christian Siligrini, Matthew Siligrini, and Austin Siligrini, to my grandchildren, Aiden Glamp, Olivia Glamp and baby RJ Glamp, and to the mothers of my grandchildren, Gianna Belfiore and Kelly Tomosky, you have all brought joy to my life. Each one of you have been blessings in my life and brought me the blessing of being a Grandmother. Each of you in your unique way has stood tall and courageous in the battle. Your care and concern for me has been one that brings comfort and light to my life. I enjoy watching each of you mature into young men and young women. May the Lord always be in your heart.

To my husband, James Siligrini, I am blessed that you were placed in my life and given to me as my helpmate, you have helped with so much more than you signed up for. Thank you for everything that you do for me and for our family. God, in His wisdom, knew I needed a strong man like you to love me, challenge me, and believe in me.

To my best friend and biggest supporter, Melissa Prickett. You have been my sunshine on cloudy days. I love how you make me smile when I want to frown. You make life better by being you. God knew our mothers could not handle us as sisters, so he made us best friends who became sisters of love. Thank you for walking this with me and for encouraging me to keep going when I doubt myself and want to give up.

To my best friend and sister in Christ, Dawn Klein. You have walked with me through the most painful time in my life, and I want to thank you for being a mom to Jimmy when I could not. Thank you for bringing Jesus Christ into his world by making it a rule that he goes to church if he's going to live with you. I know God used you in a mighty way in getting my son to see the love of Christ for him through your love for Jimmy. We will always share our sons. Wherever James was so was Jordan, and where Jordan was so was Jimmy. We both sure knew how to get to the bottom of their shenanigans didn't we?

To my pastors, Ralph Snook, Paul Scull, Tony Cotto, and TJ Shetley, each one of you have ministered to me on a level that only you can do and have been equipped to do. The Lord has really blessed each of you with the gifts of the Spirit. I showed up in your offices or on your Messenger feeds on more than one occasion to talk about what I am going through. Sometimes you had no idea I was even coming to see you but you took time out of your busy schedules to help me. You all have always shown me the love of Jesus Christ just by walking out your faith and reminding me that the real answers are found in God's Word. Each of you have encouraged me to look beyond my circumstances, look to the cross, for that is where the real victory is. I am grateful and blessed that I get to know each of you.

Introduction

This book is about my own diagnosis of bipolar disorder and the effects that it has had on me and my family. In telling my story, I hope to encourage others who suffer from this illness to live beyond the illness into wellness and wholeness. I want to encourage you to look beyond the illness and know that you can still have a meaningful and productive life. You can overcome the diagnosis and the stigma that comes with it. I hope to inspire you to reach for the heavens and into the arms of the one who can and will help you accomplish all that you dream.

Up until I received my diagnosis in the early fall months of 2009, I lived a life that was destructive. I encountered many heartbreaking and embarrassing moments. At times, I wanted to end my life because I did not see any hope. I thought that I could never rise above my situation. I hated myself for the things I did. I did not like who or what I was. In my pre-diagnosis days, all I wanted was to be liked, but I could never feel content in knowing that I was accepted and loved. I chased down moments of insanity to feel normal. I wanted purpose in life, and I wanted to make a difference, but I had to learn that the purpose I was chasing was a healthy mind, body, and soul. I found Jesus in the storm, and He showed me what my life can be if only I was to surrender.

It was at the point of surrender and laying it all down that I found the purpose I was searching for. Writing this book has taught me some things about my life. It forced me to reflect on my past behaviors and examine why I did the things I did to better understand where I have been and where I am going. My hope is that you, as the reader, will feel like you can better understand bipolar disorder from a firsthand written account.

I simply want to share my personal experience with you. Writing this book has been healing for me. It helps me to see the illness for what it is, an illness not a definition of who I am.

During my last hospital visit, I really started to dig deep into myself. Day two of my recovery from another manic episode, I wrote a poem that I would like to share with you on the next page. The poem is one of my inspirations for writing this book. I want to take you through the waves of my own storm into the light of peace and tranquility. The only source of true happiness is Jesus Christ himself.

I Lost My Mind, Where is My Hope?

Ebbed and flowed like the tide,
My mind took me for a ride.
Sometimes still and sometimes on the move,
My mind had to find its own groove.

The light house is my beacon of hope,
When anxiety is on the rise and there is no way to cope.
I look to the heavens in the sun, the moon and the stars,
I see my love, my savior Jesus and He lets me know,
It will be okay because, I did not leave my mind on Mars.

I put my hands together and pray,
And say Lord, my Father help me find my way!

Inspired by Psalms 121
-Tammy Siligrini

Part I:
Broken Apart

What Happened? Who Am I Now?

Ever since I can remember, I have felt confused on what my purpose in life was. I knew I was alive, but I did not feel like I was living my best life. In fact, I was dead on the inside. This feeling came into my life at a very early age of five years old. At five, I was molested by a friend of the family, and it tore me up inside. It broke me from within and made me feel worthless and alone. At that age, you were told to do what the adults in your life tell you to do. They were supposed to know what was best for you. But there I was standing in front of a man who was babysitting me while babysitting was not what was on his mind. The problem here was, the man whom I blindly trusted, was sick. I was confused because he told me to take my clothes off and lie on the bed. Even though I felt inside what was happening was wrong, I still complied with his demand for fear of what would happen if I said no. He told me that he was not going to hurt me and that it would be okay. This was not normal, but what could I do as a child? I closed my eyes as tight as I could and, at five years old, I allowed my mind to go somewhere other than the present situation. I had discovered disassociation for the first time in my life even if I did not know what that meant at the time. It became my defense in situations that I could not control.

I got so good at detaching myself from uncomfortable situations that it eventually became my coping method in other difficult situations. This coping method became part of the inner destruction that wrecked my life.

When he finished abusing me, he told me not to tell anyone what he did. He said if I did, no one would not believe me anyway because I was a liar and liars were not believed. As a child, I told small lies to get out of trouble, and I believed no one would believe me about this situation. So, I told no one for a long time. I tried to block that disgusting moment out of my mind, but the scene repeated itself often at nighttime when I was all by myself. I could not forget that moment I tried to escape from; in fact, it became my living nightmare. I was so scared someone would find out that I let the man hurt me and blame me for what happened.

Shame set deeply within the core of me. I kept a dark secret that chained me to brokenness. The days brought distractions from the moment in time that played over and over in my mind. I went to school as if nothing happened and secretly hoped my classmates would not find out my secret. If they knew what I was hiding, they would make fun of me and call me names. School became my only escape from the torment I was experiencing inside because, at school, no one bothered me. In fact, I started to isolate myself from others and became very lonely without friends. I thought if I did not get close to anyone, then no one would find out.

Eventually, I let the secret out and told my mother. She became so angry at the situation. I knew she was not mad at me because she told me she so. She assured me that it was not my fault, which brought some comfort. She called the police, and the matter was taken care of. But I never received any kind of counseling to help me deal with what happened to me. After the legal aspect of the event was resolved, we never mentioned it again. We buried it deep and never spoke of it again. But it did not go away. The memory of the incident morphed into something bigger later. It made me become a very promiscuous woman later in life. Eventually, I equated sex to mean love or showing love. There was a difference between the two, but it took a long time before I learned that. In fact, it took one encounter with Christ to change how I viewed a sexual relationship, but, at the time, I had yet to meet this Jesus Christ everyone talked about.

In second grade, I met one special man who saved me from complete self-destruction, though I did not always follow through on my relationship with him. In second grade, I went to a church in my hometown that I really liked because it had so many interesting activities for an eight-year-old. The church had an Awanna Club on Wednesday nights that I attended faithfully. I played games before each class with other kids I deemed better than me because they were church kids. Those kids' lives were perfect in my childlike view. I always looked at others with admiration and at myself as worthless. I believed I deserved everything I got from others. I had very low self-esteem, but at the time, I did not know what to call it. I liked these kids though. They accepted me and wanted to be my friend. I did not have many friends because I kept people at a distance and was scared of getting hurt again.

Soon, school started to become my prison. I was made fun of because of my awkward appearance and low self-esteem. No one wanted to be around the messed-up girl who had zero confidence. Church became the new place of escape for me and continued to be a place of refuge to this day. One Wednesday evening, I recited my memory verse, "For God so loved the world that he gave His only begotten Son. That whosoever believeth in Him should not perish but have everlasting life" (John 3:16, KJV). Memorizing this verse was a big deal for me because it gave me my very first patch for my vest. I said it flawlessly and was proud of myself. I asked what the verse really meant, and the leader explained it to me. She told me that if I believed in my heart that Jesus died for me and asked Him into my heart that I would be saved, and my sins forgiven. I believed that Jesus was real and that He died for me, so I asked her how to have him come into my heart. She prayed with me, and I got saved right then and there.

My belief never wavered, but my faith was tested over and over again. I failed many times. I became frustrated and walked away from church when I turned fifteen years old. I became a prodigal daughter. I wanted to do things my way and not God's way. I foolishly thought I knew better than God, and my mother, what was best for my life. I was rebellious and out of control. Looking back, I think I just wanted to have some control over things that I knew were out of control. Making my own decisions, no matter how stupid they were, was my independence and freedom, so I thought.

I met a guy who was older than me. We did everything together, including having sex. I thought that when you loved someone you simply had sex with them. Sex was not new to me, but it was my first time having a real sexual relationship with someone who cared for me. I became pregnant with my first child. There we were, my first real boyfriend and I, having a baby.

James, who we called Jimmy, was born on January 5, 1993. The moment Jimmy came into this world was amazing. His little cry melted my heart, and I experienced such a presence of God right there in the delivery room. I briefly held him in my arms. The doctors took him to the neonatal intensive care unit (NICU) because the doctors were concerned about him and wanted to keep a good eye on him. Jimmy spent the first few days of his life in the NICU. By the time I was released from the hospital, he was released from the NICU. My mind swirled with thoughts of what if something happened to him and I had to bury my first child.

At home, things started to take an awful turn. My boyfriend and I were not getting along, so we broke up. I was disappointed because I did not want to raise a baby on my own, but it became my reality. I wanted to finish high school while I still had the support of my mom at home. But my home life became difficult because I wanted to be an adult and a teenager at the same time. I had responsibilities of being a mother, and I really wanted to be a great mom and protector, but even that was messed up in my life.

I made plans to leave home with my son; however, those plans did not work out the way I had it in my mind. There was some deceit that had taken place, and

I lost custody of my son. What felt like betrayal turned to hatred. I hated my mother for such a long time because she took custody of my boy. I could not understand why she chose to hurt me the way she did. However, she did what she thought was best for Jimmy at the time. She was scared that I would not take care of him properly because I was such a young mother. God healed that part of my life, and today I have the best relationship with my mom. Forgiveness was so powerful in restoring our relationship.

I was nineteen years old when I moved into a home in Camden, New Jersey with a boyfriend who later became my fiancé. My mother had taken custody of Jimmy by the time I moved there, and that tore me up inside. I was mad at her because the courts tried to put me into a juvenile detention center when I sought custody of my son. I ran from the building because I did not want to be locked up in a detention center. I could not believe my mother wanted me locked up in a detention center for wanting to have my own life. I was angry and hurt. I did not know how to process this properly, so I started drinking heavily and smoking marijuana to take my mind off my troubles. It was at that point that I started to act like a real wild person.

I started to sneak into bars and get men to buy me drinks with the promise of going home with them. On one occasion, I was so intoxicated that I found myself waking up in a stranger's house. I was scared because I had no idea how I got there or what I did. I still do not know to this day what happened; I only know that I got out of there quickly. I took many chances that night, and I could have lost my life, but it did not stop me from taking the same risk the very next weekend. My drinking and dangerous lifestyle was taking a toll on my fiancé, and he made it very clear that we were through.

After my fiancé and I broke up, I was still living in our house because I had nowhere else to go, and I did not want to be at my mother's house. I became even worse after the breakup. I started drinking everyday instead of just on the weekends. I wanted to be out of the house as much as possible. I did not want to see him because seeing him meant that I would have to deal with the pain of a failed engagement. I drank so much one night that I got alcohol poisoning. I threw up in my sleep, and I was lucky that I did not choke on my own vomit. It was the second time I gambled with my life. Eventually, I moved from that house back into my mother's home. I spiraled out of control and wanted a change. I just did not know what it would look like.

Moving back home did not stop me from drinking and smoking pot. I continued my nightly adventures. I got a job as a janitorial worker where I waxed and stripped floors for a few hours with the boss. We often went to bars afterward because they were the only places still open to get something to eat. However, bars were the wrong place for me because I would drink while I ate. Many nights, I slept on the porch because my mother locked me out of the house. She was sick and tired of seeing her daughter coming home drunk and stumbling through the house waking up the younger children.

I talked to my boss one night and told him that I was not happy with the direction my life was going in. This was the point God stepped in and started to order my steps to recovery. My boss asked if I wanted help with my drinking and drug abuse. I told him yes. The very next day he took me to Teen Challenge. I did not know what Teen Challenge was about until I got there. I explained to the counselors that I was a mess, I was an addict in need of help, and I had gotten to a point where I did not know who I was or how to overcome this. I was accepted into the live-in program hoping a new me would emerge. Would I become the person God created me to be, or would I get frustrated and turn my back on God again?

Turbulent
Lifestyle

While in Teen Challenge, I discovered that I needed Jesus in my life, and I had to seek Him. I was so excited to start this new chapter in my life. My mother was a bit hesitant of the program because I was cut off from the rest of the world during the first phase of the program to allow for real recovery to take place. I talked to her on the phone to explain to her that it was Phase One, and I could not have visitors come to see me yet. She became so worried at that point because she thought I was in a cult and they were programming me. That was far from the truth, but she did not know it. I had to cut off the people, places, and things that I did when I was in my addiction. She still was not buying it, so she sent one of the deacons, Mr. Willis, from my childhood church to check out the program and get me out of there if he had to.

Mr. Willis was my favorite person from church. He was the bus captain for the church bus that picked me up as a kid. He was like a spiritual dad to me. I trusted him. He would pick me up on the bus for church every Sunday. To have a familiar face visit me in Teen Challenge was the best part of that day. They had made an exception and let him visit me because he explained my mother's concerns. I remember that day he handed me a bible inscribe with 2 Timothy 2:15 (KJV), "Study to shew thyself approved unto God, a workman that needeth not to be ashamed, rightly dividing the word of truth." I read and re-read this verse over and over. It meant a lot that someone would take time out of their day to come see me and make sure that I was okay and not in a place that could destroy me. My mother's fears were put to rest after his visit.

Mr. Willis kept in touch with me over the course of my time in Teen Challenge. Mr. Willis has since gone home to be with the Lord. He was a good man who loved kids. He was one of the kindest most giving people I knew. He was the first man in my life that only loved me for me. He treated me with respect and treated me as if I was his daughter. It was his love for Jesus Christ that taught me what it means to love like Jesus. His heart for evangelism rubbed off on me. It was because of him that I love to witness to others about Jesus, and God allowed me to cross paths with this man for a reason. I needed to know that not all men were bad and wanted to take from me or abuse me. I developed a mindset at the time that the only thing men wanted from me was my body. Mr. Willis never violated my trust. In fact, he was the first man in my life I ever trusted.

After three months in Teen Challenge, I became very sick with a high fever. I was burning up and thinking to myself, *Oh great, I am going to die from the consequences from my past behaviors.* They sent me to the doctor to get medically cleared. It was at that appointment that I found out that I was pregnant with my second child, Robert. Teen Challenge explained to me that I could remain in the program until his birth. I could stay in the program after the birth if I gave a family member temporary custody. At that time, I made a bad decision to leave the program. I was afraid to give my mom custody of another son. She was already raising one son, and I did not want to give her my other one, so I packed my bags and went back home.

It was at home that I realized I did not know who my baby's father was. I could not for the life of me remember anything from my drinking days. This caused so much stress in my life. I later found out who it was and later contacted with him. I was relieved to find out who Bobby's dad was. I made that phone call thirteen years after Bobby was born to tell a man I had not spoken to in all those years that he had a son. Needless to say, he hung up on me. If it was not for his girlfriend telling him he had to call me back, I do not know if I would have ever found out. We had a DNA test done to confirm he was the father. I felt shame in my behavior but not ever in my son.

Bobby was born December 27, 1996. Two days after Christmas my little bundle arrived. My heart melted with love when I saw his little face looking up at me. I thought to myself that I had to do what was right for this little boy. I had to stay clean. No drugs or alcohol. The determination quickly faded when we got home from the hospital. I was out drinking again. I could not help myself. It started out as an innocent drink then led to more and more. I could not stop drinking. I partied so much. I just was not learning my lesson. Drinking was not my friend, but it helped to block out the pain I felt in my life. It buried the memories and I felt if I drank enough, they would go away altogether.

I drank to be cool and fit in. Everyone else was doing it too. I did not want to be left out, so I joined in. My friends all wanted to hang out, and I was more than willing. The thing is the more I drank the more I hated myself for not staying in the program, so I drank more. It became a vicious cycle of self-destruction. I was feeling like there was something wrong with me and wondered what it was. It would be thirteen more years of this up and down attempt at a normal life before I would have the answer.

I went through periods of very high highs and super low lows. There was no happy medium for me. When I experienced the lows, I would want to sleep all day and do nothing. When I was on a high elevated mood, I would stay up for days at a time doing whatever was in my mind to do. My body felt it, and I would crash. I did not hold a job for longer than nine months. I changed jobs often because I would get bored and want to move on to something new. I got mad at people for not knowing what was going on in my head. I criticized everyone for not knowing how I felt. It was a false misdirection of my own anger and frustration with myself. I was not a pleasant person to be around.

I got a job as a cashier for McDonalds. I needed a job, and they were hiring. It was there that I met my husband. One day while getting drinks after work, I was talking to a coworker. While sitting at the bar, I said to my friend that I thought Jim was cute. He had been flirting with me at work, and I started flirting back after some time. My friend took me to her friend's house where Jim was. I did not know what she was up to until it was too late. Not long after we arrived at her friend's house, she told me she had to go do something really quick and would be back to pick me up. She asked me if I was alright staying there without her. I told her it was fine. She never came back to pick me up, so I had to ask Jim to take me home. That night he asked me to go on a date with him. I said yes. The next day we went to Atlantic City to eat dinner and sit on the beach. We talked all night on the beach. It got really late, so he took me home. He asked if I would be his girlfriend, and I said yes. I was already liking him, so we started dating after that night.

I made a decision to not have a sexual relationship with him. He was the first guy that I decided to wait to have a sexual relationship with. Something about him was different, and in my very being, I knew he was someone I want to know more about. We spent months getting to know each other. We spent a lot of time at the beach or going to baseball games or eating dinner. He became a man I wanted to spend the rest of my life with. I wanted someone stable in my life, and he was that man. He was completely opposite of me. He was responsible; I was not. We started to grow as a couple. We did everything together. Eventually we had our first baby together.

Joseph was born June 30, 1999. We knew we wanted to be a family. Jim and I cried the day that Joey was born. He had experienced the love of God for the first time. There was something about bringing a life into the world that made me become very aware that there was a God. Three years later, we were married. We said

"I do" on January 16, 2002. It was on our wedding night that we conceived our second son, Christian. He came into the world on September 12, 2002.

I was excited to start a family with someone who loved me as much as I loved him. The thing is as much as I loved him, I could not keep from wanting to party. I left Jim home most nights to care for the children while I partied. I was so unpredictable at the time, and it frustrated Jim to no end. I stayed out all night and would not come home until the sun came up. When I got home, we would fight about where I was and what I was doing. I never had any real answer to give him other than excuses for why I did not come home. One year, we were fighting so bad that I threw the Christmas tree out of the front door. It was the most horrible thing I could do to my family. I did not know how the tree ended up in my hands, but before I knew it, the tree was flying out the front door with my marriage.

Jim and I separated. I had freedom to do whatever I wanted, and that freedom came with a huge cost. My children suffered, and my husband was left to pick up the pieces. We repeated this pattern on three more occasions. We would fight, and I would leave. I would come back, and things would be fine for a few months to a year, and we would be back at it. It was not healthy for any of us, especially the children. Each time I left and came back, we had a child. Matthew was born on

June 6, 2005, and Austin was born on August 8, 2008. Looking at the timing of their births and the pattern I was continuing, I knew something was not right, but I could not put my finger on it yet. I did not realize it at the time, but it was my pattern of cycling through depression and mania.

When I was depressed, I was home in isolation with just my family, but then after some time it was as if something suddenly switched in my brain and I wanted to be around everyone to get out of my funky feeling and live again. The problem was that I overwhelmed myself with massive plans to do everything I was putting off, plus the new stuff my mind was making up to do.

Jim was trying to figure out what he was doing wrong and why his wife was so unpredictable. He did not know what was really happening with me. He was feeling rejected at times by me. I caused pain in his life. I also created a great deal of problems between him and me. He was not happy, and he let me know he was not happy. On more than one occasion he said he wanted a divorce and could not take it anymore. I was devastated because I did not want a divorce to break up my relationship and my family. We both were at our wits end with each other. I did not know if we were going to make it. What was it going to take to fix this?

The Diagnosis

In 2009, I found myself sitting in my car disgusted with my life, my family, and my uncontrolled behavior. My two oldest children were cutting school, and my husband hated me for the things I was doing. My inconsistency in parenting was taking a toll on my children and causing a major rift between Jim and me. We were not happy. The thought occurred to me to drive myself off the Walt Whitman bridge. I felt like everyone in my life would be better off without me. It was with that very thought that I knew I was in trouble. It was the first time I had a plan to end my life. I had thought about dying before, but I never had a plan. This time I did, and the urge to end it all was strong within me. I was tired of the pain I was causing. My children were acting out because I was not providing a stable home. How could I? I was not stable, and I did not know how to get stable. I could not help myself in what I was doing. The drinking and drugs were taking a toll on me and only masking the real issues. I could not keep up with the turbulent lifestyle I was living.

I decided it was time to put my past behind me and get some help. Where was I to turn for the help I needed? I started praying and asking God for help. I told him that I really did not want to kill myself, I just wanted the rollercoaster to stop so I could get off of it. I started searching for answers for real. It was at this time we were losing our first home, so my stress level was at an all-time high. Something snapped inside of my mind. The stress of it all came crashing down on me like a ton of bricks weighing me down. My mind decided to create a false reality.

There I was on the front porch telling Jim, Jimmy, and my mother that they all needed Jesus. I was deflecting big time. I was the one who really needed Jesus at that time. They did too, but it was my turn to start this process of redemption, and I needed Jesus to help me get my life in order. On this particular night, I stayed up reading my bible. I was searching for the answer to my problems. I could not find the answers I was looking for and became even more frustrated. I wanted a quick fix, but that was not what I needed. I searched for days on end. I went to several different pastors and churches looking for answers, and each one of them told me to seek the Kingdom of God and all things will be added unto you. I had no idea what they were talking about, so it frustrated me more. I did not want all things; I just wanted normal and steady. I wanted to be a whole person not a fragmented individual.

At one point in my battle, I baptized myself in our large bathtub. Jim came into the bathroom to find me in my clothes soaking wet. He asked what I was doing, and I told him I baptized myself. He jokingly said, "Who do you think you are, Jesus?" I looked at him dumbfounded but convinced that yes, indeed, I was Jesus Christ in the flesh. He told me to go get some sleep because I was not making sense. Little did I know Jim found out I was walking around in my bathrobe in the backyard earlier that day talking to no one. I might have been praying, but I do not know because it was in the early morning the previous day when my mind started to create that false reality. I went to lie down to appease Jim. It was around two or three in the morning when I started to get restless in bed, and I jumped to my feet to pray again. I thought the devil was in my basement, so I flung open the door and started yelling for him to leave now. It was at this moment that I woke up Jim from a deep sleep with my yelling and praying in tongues. He could not reason with me. I kept telling him that he was the devil and he had to leave. He called my mother because he had no idea what to do to get me to calm down. I scared him so terribly because he had never seen me in that condition before. I had never seen myself in that condition ever before either. My mom and my sister, Paula, came to the house to find out what was going on. They called the ambulance to come take me to the hospital. Jim was terrified that I was going to remain insane for the rest of my life. He did not know what was going on. All he knew was that I was not acting like myself and I needed help.

The police arrived at my house first. My mother intercepted the cops outside to tell them what was going on; while in the bedroom, Paula was helping me get dressed from my bed clothes to normal clothing. She was brushing my hair when the cops showed up in the doorway. Paula was the only one I would let near me at that time. I think the stroke of the brush against my head started to calm me down to a certain degree. Paula coached me into the ambulance by telling me that my people needed to see me because, at this point, I was Jesus in my mind.

The ride to the hospital was one of the worst rides I ever took. The chemistry in my brain was way off, and what I needed was medication and not the EMTs making fun of me to my face as if this was amusing to them. They kept talking about the devil. One guy told me that he was the devil. I panicked at his words because at the time it became real to me. I believed everything that he was saying, and again, I started yelling at the top of my lungs telling him to go back to hell where he belonged.

When we arrived at the hospital, they put me in a room with only a bed in it. I became hard to care for because I thought the world was ending that night, so they gave me medicine to knock me out for the night. However, it did not work because I went into other patients' rooms to pray for them. My world, as I knew it, was ending because this was the beginning of awareness that something other than my addiction was wrong. They brought me back to my room, gave me more medicine, and put a heart monitor on me. I thought they were trying to kill me, so I ripped the IV out of my arm. Luckily, a nurse was posted to my door to keep me in the room because I was bleeding all over the place. They were able to stop the bleeding and put a new IV in but not before I attacked the male nurse. He was holding me down to keep me still so they could stop the bleeding. Somehow, my other hand got free, and I pulled a necklace from the nurse's neck. In my false reality, they were trying to crucify me like they did to the real Jesus. Only in my version, it was modernized with an IV bag and heart monitor instead of a cross and nails.

I fell asleep and woke up in another hospital room. The room was very dark when I opened my eyes. At first, I thought I was in hell and began to panic some. That was until my roommate turned in her bed to see the new person she had to share a room with. Then I realized I was in the crisis unit wing of the hospital.

I really felt confused about what had taken place. My mind was trying to recall pieces of memory from the previous day and night to put together a full picture of what happened; however, the number of drugs in my system made everything foggy and unfocused. I was a little afraid to move from my bed because I was not sure I was allowed. I had a vague memory of the nurses in the emergency room telling me that if I did not stay in my bed they would to tie me to my bed. I, in turn, became focused on basic survival mode. I was only really concerned with eating and sleeping for the first few days. I worked up the courage to ask the nurse on duty if I could eat. I felt like the worst that could happen is that they would tie me to my bed, but I was so hungry I needed to take the chance and ask for some food. I walked to the nurse's station to find someone. The nurse was very nice, and she told me she could get me a sandwich until the next meal time where I can have a full meal. I felt like crying because I felt like I was stripped of all my dignity and I had to ask permission for certain things. I was so confused from the psychoactive drugs. I thought I better ask to go to the bathroom too, and that was when I lost it. The tears flowed down my cheeks as if a river of emotions were raging. I was completely broken!

It was in this brokenness that I found the real God. The one who created me. The one who I believed knew how to break my strong will just enough to have me see my nakedness of sin. I evaluated everything in my life previously and, with His help, realized this was the very beginning I needed and was longing for. What I thought was dead inside was actually coming to life, but the process would be a long but rewarding process. I just did not know it at the time that this was my redemption. I just could not see that far down the path just yet. Some work needed to be put in, and the first step was for me to accept what is about to happen.

The Hospital Visit

On the first night I knew I was staying and not getting out anytime soon, I was agitated. I could not leave even if I wanted to because I was declared a risk to myself and others. I had to wait for the doctor to mentally clear me to leave the hospital. That first night was hard for me to be away from my family. I missed them and wanted to assure them that I was okay and doing better even though I was not better. My mind was still cloudy from the medications they gave me in the emergency room. I was a bit scared. I had never been on the mental side of the hospital before, and I did not know what to expect. For most people, it is a scary thought to be locked on a floor with other mental patients, but I can assure you that they were harmless. We all had one goal, and that was to get better and go home.

I spent eight days in the crisis unit getting better with each new day. But my mind was broken into what felt like a million fragmented pieces. All I wanted to do was pull back those missing fragments and make myself whole again. I could not do common things like hold a simple conversation. Everything that came out of my mouth was broken into incomplete, random thoughts. I was afraid that I would be left in this condition, a shell of my old self, and my life as I once knew it as would be over. I could not get a routine going for myself for a few days, but with each new day, I was able to work something new into my day like asking for a notebook and pencil to write down my thoughts and questions as they came to me. This was beneficial to my recovery. It was an important step in helping me to be more active in my care. I used that notebook to talk to my doctor during visits. There was so much to cover in a fifteen-minute conversation, and it took me a good fifteen minutes the first few days to realize he was the doctor that would determine whether I was to remain in the hospital or be released. I was determined to get my thoughts across even if I had to read from that notebook what I was thinking about all day before seeing my doctor.

Each day, we had to give ourselves goals. My goal always remained the same: go home to my family well. I did not like the crisis unit even if it was helping me. I felt like I was under constant scrutiny, and I had to explain my feelings but that was the point though. I had to explore those things because hiding and masking them was what made me broken to begin with. I buried my feelings so deep that one day they exploded all over my life and my family's lives too.

It was then that I was diagnosed with bipolar depression disorder. When the doctor revealed to me the diagnosis, I felt my surroundings shift and swirl around me. I first thought after that, *Great now, I am certifiably crazy.* My family already thought I was a mess, and now they had a piece of paper to hold in my face to say I told you so. The reality of it was my family was just as devastated by the diagnosis as I was, but at least now we had an answer.

The doctor put me on several different medications for bipolar, sleep, and anxiety. I did not like how the medicine made me feel. I did not feel like me. Maybe it meant that I was not the same wild person I was before, so I had to adjust to the new me.

Something strange but good happened in the crisis unit.. I found out that I was not that different from everyone else. We all had a misconception on what life should look like. It was as if someone told us all the same lie and we believed it. The lie was that we were the only ones who coped with life in unhealthy ways and we could never be accepted as we were. I felt more accepted in the hospital than surrounded by my family and friends. It seemed as though everyone in my life had changed the way they interacted with me when they found out I had a mental health issue. In the hospital, we listened to each other and encouraged each other to get better without making each other feel like we were being judged for something we had no control over yet. The unit was like its own village taking care of its members. If one person was down, then the group would make it their mission to help that person as much as they can. We developed friendships in there. It was important to us to make everyone part of the group because in the group setting, we were more honest with ourselves and each other. Someone would bring something up in the group therapy and others would respond with similar experiences.

I went to therapy sessions throughout the day. Music therapy and art therapy were available. In the beginning, I did not want to attend those therapies, but eventually I saw the benefit in them by allowing me to go through the process and open up. I guess at some point I really did not care if I was horrible at drawing or playing an instrument, I just wanted to complete their sessions so they could evaluate me and send me home. I no longer cared what the other patients thought of me as well. I figured I might as well just open up and move forward. I remember one girl in the hospital with me who was feeling the same things I was. She was shy and was not opening up either. When I started to reveal what I was feeling, she decided to find comfort in knowing she was not alone, and she seemed to come alive to me. In the days prior, she was quiet and withdrawn, but then she seemed to bounce back to life, smiling and talking to not only me but the group and the staff.

Art therapy became my favorite group to participate in because I liked to paint and express myself through my creation. In art therapy, we were asked to draw a picture of ourselves in the rain. I drew a picture of me playing in the rain. We analyzed each other's drawings. The art therapy counselor told me that she was concerned because I did not have protection from the rain which represented that I did not have protection in reality. I did not agree with her assessment because I had the love and protection at home. Jim was, and still is, my biggest protector. I had to explain to her that the rain was a good memory I was trying to recall. When I was a kid, I enjoyed playing in the rain. It felt good on my skin in the summertime. I loved being outside enjoying the outdoors. The mud puddles were the best to play in because it was my own little pond where I felt free and safe. I was trying to recapture my childhood though I had no idea why because my childhood was not at all good. It had its own challenges, but I do have some great memories of fun and connection. One fond memory is when my mom decided we were going to have a water fight in the house. We grabbed cups of water from the sink and would pour it on each other. Water was everywhere. We had so much fun though the apartment was drenched, and eventually we had to stop playing and start cleaning. I am not sure, but I suspect the apartment below us had some water seeping through, and that was why we had to stop having our water fight and start cleaning our mess up. Even cleaning up the water was fun. We laughed about what we had just did. It was against the rules, and we broke those rules with permission and participation from Mom.

I did not like the music therapy at first. The songs that played were bit worldly and dark. I could not handle the depressing songs that some chose to listen to. I asked to speak to the counselor outside the room to explain to him why I did not want to participate. I did not feel it appropriate for me to discuss my personal concerns and feelings about the music choices in front of the group. I did not want to hurt anyone's feelings or make enemies. He told me that if I did not participate that it would not look good for me. After explaining to him why I did not want to participate, we came to an agreement that I would sit in the group without saying anything and in the next session, the counselor would choose something different for the entire group to participate in.

The counselor brought in some instruments for the next session. He asked us to choose an instrument that spoke to us. I chose a drum to tap on. I felt like a warrior and like I was in a fight for my freedom, so I figured I would sound the feelings I was having about my situation. The sound penetrated the chest and went into the soul. One person would start playing their instrument and as we felt the need to join in, we would. It was beautiful because we made music together in each of our brokenness. It was beautiful to hear. Each one of us let the emotions flow through our choices of instruments. It was like God was showing me that when we cry out to Him, our brokenness was a beautiful melody to Him because He already knows the plan of redemption for us. Someday, I would like to learn to play the guitar so I can create a song from my heart for my Lord and Savior. I started by getting a reasonably priced guitar to play around with. Often, I have found myself looking up videos of how to play the guitar and try to mimic the hand positions. The different sounds my hands made while strumming sound beautiful and peaceful to my ears in stressful times. It was a tool in my wellness toolbox for staying healthy in my mind.

After about eight days of therapy and medication, I was released from the hospital. It was a bittersweet moment. I wanted to be home, but I knew I would miss my group. We had bonded, and I did not want to leave that behind, but I knew I had to go so I can unpack everything I acquired in the hospital for maintaining my wellness. Jim picked me up from the hospital unsure of what to expect. He was my buffer in making sure that my stress levels did not rise up on me. He would keep people away who he thought would bring stress and negativity into my life. Still to this day, he is protective of me. Now when my stress levels are on the rise, he will send me packing to my best friend's house to get away from home and family stress.

Sometimes, I took advantage of it and went just to spend time with my best friend, Melissa. Other times, I simply said I was going to push through the difficulties. Melissa and I have been friends for more than twenty years. Melissa never judged me but instead loved me where I was. I loved her just as unconditionally. God knew what He was doing when He sent her into my life. Melissa and Jim were, and are, both my advocates and part of my accountability group when it comes to my mental health. I trusted both of them completely, and I knew they would only do what is best for me when I could not make my own decisions for myself. And I knew that they both love me deeply. God really showed me what real love was through the both of them.

During my last hospital stay, Melissa came to visit me. It was the first time she saw me in that state. I never let anyone visit me before, but this was different. I wanted her and Jim to visit as much as they possibly could. I felt like familiar faces would help me recover quicker than previous hospital visits. My theory worked for me, and I was released days earlier than previous visits. Melissa was taken aback by what it was like in there. It was the first time she was in the mental health unit of the hospital. I assured her that I was okay, and I would be fine. Being my best friend, she jokingly said that wanted to sneak me out of there. That was my best friend, always looking out for me. If it was the other way around, I would have tried to do the same thing just because I love her so much. She understood that for me to get well I had to remain where I was, and she encouraged me to participate as much as I could so I can be released. We had an important mission of taking a long road trip somewhere to clear our minds and enjoy the open road. Friends, she is my road trip buddy. We have logged so many miles together and so much more memorable moments together. I have always said if you have just one faithful and true friend in this world you have everything. She truly is a genuine, kindhearted person. I am so blessed that God brought her into my life some twenty years ago.

Part II:
The Healing of My Mind

The Pastor's Office

There was one incident that happened in church that I will never forget. I am truly embarrassed by it, but it has to be told. During a service, I was listening to a speaker talking about Queen Esther and the story of Haman plotting to destry the Jews. Queen Esther was a Jew, and her uncle, Mordecai, was favored by Persian King Ahasuerus because Mordecai had saved Ahasuerus' life. Queen Esther fasted and prayed before going to the king to tell him what Haman was up to.

As I was sitting there, I thought to myself that I felt like an Esther who had been praying for a breakthrough my life was on the line, but I was not seeing the results of my prayers. I know now that things do not get done on my timeline but on God's timeline. During that service, there was an alter call for prayer, so I went to the front of the church to receive an Esther anointing prayer. I wanted to be like Esther and have all her characteristics and qualities. Instead what came out of my mouth that night was not what Esther would say. I still had a foul mouth, and my favorite word at that time was the F-word. I used that word in front of the whole church congregation. I do not know how many people there were to witness it, but I do know that is when I became good friends with Pastor Tony. I ended up spending a lot of time in his office talking about my mental issues.

Pastor Tony recognized the episode for what it was: a psychotic break in my mind. He helped Jim get me out of the church so Jim could take me to get help. When I was released from the hospital this time, Pastor Tony invited Jim and I into his office to talk about what had happened. There was no scolding or making me feel worse than I already felt; instead, Pastor Tony said to us that he loved us and wanted us at the church. I really needed to hear that. If not for those words of acceptance of me, I do not know where I would be today. Pastor Tony offered to counsel Jim and me and to help us through this difficult time. Jim needed as much of a friend in this as I did because he was just as torn apart as I was. My pastor knew he did not have to sugar coat anything with me. He told me the truth like it was, even if it was not something I wanted to hear. He helped me understand it though. God really blessed him with compassion and love. He was the first pastor in my life who

I felt I could be myself with, and I could tell him all of the things I did not feel comfortable telling anyone else.

I often showed up to church during the week without an appointment to talk to Pastor Tony. He would take time out of his busy day to talk me through whatever crisis I thought I was going through. Most times it was because Jim and I were arguing about my illness. I wanted to do things my way, and Jim just wanted things done that were healthy for me, like avoid stress. I would bring these things to Pastor Tony, and he would not take sides. However, he had a way of helping me see things from Jim's point of view while also validating my feelings. I was able to walk out of those meetings with a better perspective and attitude towards Jim. I also learned to not just show up at the church but to call and make an appointment so I do not interrupt my pastor's schedule. I learned that my moods and emotions will change sometimes several times during any given day. I did not have to react to the moment but rather give that moment to God and talk to him about it first. It was good to be respectful of others time, but I knew that if I needed my pastor, he would be there to help me.

There was another occasion where I was in Pastor Paul's office. Pastor Paul was one of the pastors at my church who was in charge of Turning Point Ministry. Turning Point was a ministry for inner healing deliverance and counseling. Ordained ministers and lay counselors were trained to help individuals and married couples with issues such as depression, anxiety, anger issues, marital problems and spiritual issues. I was struggling with the memory of being molested as a child. I prayed and asked God for help because I wanted to overcome this and be healed. I felt like God said this was the moment we were going to deal with the traumas of the past, and God was going to use Pastor Paul to take me through inner healing.

I sat in Pastor Paul's office unsure of what to expect. I was nervous to let go of the secret I kept to only a few people and myself. I was about to tell the pastor what happened to me as a young girl. My insides started to shake from within, and in a childlike voice, I explained what happened so many years ago. It was as if I was five years old again. I told him I just wanted to be free from that whole experience and I did not want what happened to have power anymore. With tears rolling down my cheeks and a soggy tissue in my hand, I joined in prayer with Pastor Paul. He bound the enemy and asked the Holy Spirit to show me what happened in that moment. Pastor Paul asked me to close my eyes and go back to that moment. He asked me where Jesus was in that time. I looked around in the room, and I could not see Jesus. Pastor Paul once again bound the enemy and asked me to look again in that memory for

Jesus. To my surprise, I saw Him. My Lord was crying at the sight of this grown man abusing me. Then I saw, in this memory vision, Jesus pushing this man off of me. As He was pushing this man off, so was I. Although this did not take place in the natural realm, I believed it did within the supernatural realm of the moment. Once I realized that Jesus was there in that moment, a floodgate of healing tears started to flow like a river. I was sobbing and had mucus running from my nose, but the best part was that I felt a great weight lift from my body. Until that moment, I had not realized this invisible weight burdened me, but then, I felt the freedom from it. Not only was weight lifted, but the chain that tied me to my abuser was broken as well. I was free just like Jesus said I would be in His word if I would only trust in Him.

Now that I got a taste of what real freedom in Jesus meant, I knew I wanted more of it. Although I journaled before then, I began to journal about everything as the Holy Spirit brought it to the forefront of my mind. Each time I journaled those painful memories, I asked the Lord to show me where He was in it all. Each time, faithfully the Holy Spirit showed me a picture of whatever would bring healing to my mind. The memories of trauma I endured in my lifetime no longer had the same power it did before. Instead, when the enemy tried to remind me of my shame, I was able to say to the enemy

"Get behind me because that memory has been covered by my Lord and Savior Jesus Christ." Those memories no longer held me captive in depressive thoughts because each time they come up, I thought on what the Holy Spirit showed me and what the word of God said.

One of my favorite verses to think upon was "For He hath not given us a spirit of fear but of power, of love and a sound mind" (2 Timothy 1:7, KJV). I thought so much on the "sound mind" part because I wanted that so much, and I did not realize I had power and love too. Our God is so great that he not only gave us a sound mind but power and love to face our trials courageously in Him. Holy Spirit is the power, our guide in this evil world to overcome the schemes of the enemy that try to hold us captive in sin and shame. Love is what we are promised from our Father. He loves us so much that he sends us help in our time of need. For me, it was my husband, my children, my friends, and my Pastors. God knew that moment in time where it would all come to a crossroad, and He already had a plan to get me out of that darkness and into the light of His love. He knew who He was going to use those people and they would be faithful in helping me achieve success in my quest for wholeness. There is a verse that says "He will never leave you nor forsake you" (Deuteronomy 31:6, NIV). That promise has never been broken in my life. Even in the moments when I felt all alone, I was not alone;

my God was with me and working on my behalf. And I would have to remember this when my life was about to take a turn that I was not expecting.

Do I Have Bipolar?

I had an incident that convinced me I had the correct diagnosis. Prior to that, I was not sure if this was the right diagnosis or if I should even be on medications. My brain was lying to me and telling me I was okay when I was not, so I stopped taking my medications. I discussed this with my doctor, and he agreed to wean me down and take me off the medications to see if I would have another incident. I was still learning about bipolar disorder, but I did not want to be the one who had it. I had my own personal stigmas to overcome, but I was not there yet.

After completely stopping the medications, I did very well for almost three years. I had no incidents. I really thought they had diagnosed me wrong. I won, or at least I thought I did, but again in the fall months, I got depressed and was looking for a way to combat the feelings. My brain flipped a switch inside me, and all of a sudden, I was going to become the mother of the year. I was a stay at home mom because I could not work.

Since I was not working, I decided I wanted to be the best mom ever and make up for all the things my children went through in prior years. I was dedicated to the point of exhaustion, mentally and physically.

During the 2016 presidential election, I started staying up late watching the news and reading news articles obsessively. I was concerned for who I was going to vote for. I did not want to choose anyone on the ballot, but I had to choose someone. I did not want to cast a vote that would leave my children with the consequences in the future, so I was doing my homework too diligently. I was not sleeping well, and most times, I was too preoccupied to even eat one small meal let alone three of them. My brain was telling me all sorts of things during this period. Things like "I was going to run out of time" or "I was sure to mess things up for my kids if I did not pay attention and get it right." Then there was the imaginary mom of year award I was determined to win.

One evening, I lied down on the couch to get some rest. I was tired and knew I needed some sleep. So, I figured I would take a nap. Then, my phone rang, and I answered it. Robert needed a ride home from work. I told him that I would pick him up even though my body was screaming for rest. I jumped in the car with the other kids. I arrived at his job only to have to wait for him to get back to the shop. No big deal, I thought; however, it took longer than both of us knew. I was looking at the clouds when a voice from within me said, "Do you see the size of those clouds?" I looked intensely at the clouds, and they looked like a really huge dragon sweeping across the sky. I wondered what this was about. I heard the voice within me say, "Those clouds are a representation of the spirit that has a stronghold over this nation, do you think you are strong enough to handle that?" I replied to myself and said, "No, that thing is huge. I do not want any parts of battling that demon." I forgot about that for the moment as Robert pulled up with his coworkers. He hopped into the car, and we took off. I started to get extremely tired, so I asked Robert to drive us home. My eyes felt like led. I was dozing off periodically. We finally made our way home. It was about that time when I got my second wind, and I felt wide awake. I was pushing myself too hard to care for a family by myself, and I was not letting my husband help.

While at home, I remembered that I had to get a birthday present for my neighbor's child. So, I told the kids to pile in the car to go get the gift. A simple five-minute car ride turned into hours of driving across New Jersey from the Atlantic City area to Northern New Jersey by New York. Somehow, I got lost in the state I grew up in when the store was only five minutes from my house. It was not a simple getting lost; it was exhaustion, and my brain was not functioning at all. My husband, Jim, became worried about me because I was not answering my phone. I was driving, and I could not talk on the phone. I really wanted to just get home with the kids. Jim was overreacting by calling me over fifty times in an hour. In his defense, he had no idea what was going on other than I was lost and could not find my way home. Then things got really weird. My own brain turned against me and convinced me that I was the Holy Spirit. In my past when I became delusional, I convinced myself I was Jesus Christ. So, being the Holy Spirit was something very new. I could not look at my children or other people for fear that I would see their true sinful nature and bring instant judgment on them. I told my son, Christian, to get in the front seat so he can be my eyes and help us get home. I covered my eyes and took the wheel to drive us home. I cannot imagine what my son felt at that moment other than real fear. I am supposed to protect these children not put them in danger, and there I was putting them in danger. On the positive side, I recognized that he could not do it so I parked at a stop light and went to sleep. I thought I was parked on the side of the street, but, like I said, I was exhausted and knew I needed sleep.

I awoke to the police opening the door and asking questions about why I was at a red light sleeping. I had not realized that I was sleeping at or even parked at a red light. All four of us were sleeping in the car. The police officer asked if I had been drinking, and I had answered him in gibberish. I had just woken up, and I was in the middle of a dream and awake at the same time. I spoke to him in an unknown tongue. It was at that point when they realized I needed medical attention not police intervention, so they called the ambulance. The ambulance took me medical center for observation. My mind could not understand why the police officers did not know what I was saying. I was confronted with the reality that I was not the Holy Spirit, but it would still be days before my right mind would come back to me because I was put on some powerful medications.

At the hospital, I was taken to the crisis unit. I was "locked" in a small room that had a TV in it but nothing else. The door really was not locked just shut, but my mind locked it forever. I did not watch much TV because my mind was still processing what was real and what was not real. The staff thought it was quite entertaining until I shoved my hand under the door and "locked" myself in the room. One compassionate nurse came over to me and said that she needed to get into the room, and she wanted to know what she had to do to get into the room. I told her to tap my hand and that would unlock the door. She tapped my hand lightly, and I let go of the bottom of the door and let her in. They brought me some food to eat. I remember sitting in a chair eating my food. Sometime later, they took me to the unit where I got a regular room.

I woke up the next day shattered. Reality had returned to me. I was faced with the fact that my mind was shattered yet again, and I was in the hospital. I had no choice but to accept that I was sick and needed help. I surrendered again to an illness I had no control over. I had a notebook to write things down because the medications affected my short-term memory. I wrote down everything and anything that came to my mind. I used this information to help me get better. I read my notes every night to remember my day. At one point, I noticed the clock and the weekly schedule of group meetings on the wall. It was as if I was waking from a dream. I knew from the last visit to the hospital that if I wanted to get out of there then I had to participate in the groups. I formed a routine quickly. I woke up in the morning, made my bed, and took a shower. After my shower, I gathered my dirty clothes and took them to the staff to be washed. I then walked the hallway for exercise while the other patients slept. When the day room opened up, I watched the news and read my bible or the newspaper. After breakfast, I attended group meetings. These groups helped me to clarify the things that were going on for me. Simple feelings and thoughts became clear and more quickly than in previous hospital visits. I suppose I had been down this road before and knew what I had to do.

On the day I was released, I did not feel like I was defeated. Instead a new determination rose within me to find how I can keep this cycle from repeating over and over again. I decided that I was going to find someone who I could talk to openly without fear of being locked away. Being locked away forever was the biggest fear that I had to overcome. I found a woman who was a Psychiatric Advance Practice Nurse (APN). The Psychiatric APN provided evaluations and prescribed medications as well as conducted counseling services for patients under the direction and supervision of a psychiatrist. My first visit with her was interesting. I was having some issues with overextending myself and taking on more responsibilities than I could handle. I was stressed out and angry at everyone but most of all Jim. I seemed to direct most of my anger at Jim. In my mind, I wanted him to just understand, but I was not able to communicate to him that I was stretched to my limits and wanted to escape. Winning that imaginary mom award was taking its toll on me, and I had to give it up. I could not be perfect. and I made mistakes. I told my APN everything that was going on. I told her how I felt my husband expected way too much from me and how my kids expected way too much from me as well, more so my adult children than my under-eighteen children. The thing was, I did not know how to say no without feeling guilty. I felt like if I said yes all the time, it meant that I was a good mom and a good wife. That was a lie because doing things for my family all the time did not make me a good wife and mother. Sometimes saying no because I was overdoing it was a good thing. It meant that I was caring for my needs so I do not wear myself out and be ineffective for my family. I do not know when I started to believe the lie of being perfect but trying to be was tearing me apart. It was an adjustment for my family to understand that I needed some time for myself. Some days it was a challenge to take thirty minutes to an hour of being unavailable to everyone, but I knew I needed to do it to have balance in my life. In the beginning, it was weird to me. I did not know what to do, but now I look forward to being, in a sense, selfish with my time.

Part III:
Is This For Real?

I Am Healed

Am I healed? A question I asked myself over and over again. I did not fully understand what healing was. In my mind, I thought being healed meant that I did not have bipolar disorder or PTSD any longer. However, God in His infinite wisdom showed me that my healing meant I could live well in spite of the diagnosis. It meant that I was not going to fold and let the diagnosis overcome me. Jesus was the ultimate overcomer and He taught me a lesson in overcoming the things that tried to hold me back from being everything God created me to be. The drugs, alcohol, and indiscriminate sex was no longer a way of life for me. It made sense that all of those things were harming me and making me feel even worse about myself. The starting point of recovery for me was to finally rid myself of the things I was doing by accepting the diagnosis. I felt like I deserved everything I had coming to me because I did these things. I was living one big fat lie, and I believed those lies until I got serious about my relationship with Jesus Christ.

Someone came into my life and brought the power of the Holy Spirit with her. Dawn was not shy or intimidated by my ways. In fact, she prayed for me and told to me everything that the Holy Spirit was revealing to her about my life. One day, I was at her house having some coffee and cake, we did that often, she looked at me and started talking about abortion. I was floored. I did not know what to say. I wanted to gulp down my coffee and stuff my mouth full of cake just to get out of there because I did not want her to know that I myself had an abortion. I carried that awful feeling with me everywhere. I just did not realize I was hiding my shame so deeply that it was really a tender and raw wound. Instead of running, I held my head in shame and started telling her my story. I told her how I had an abortion because I was abused, and my abuser got me pregnant. I told her that I was ashamed of my decision, and I thought about the life I took so often. As the tears streamed down my face, she took hold of me and started praying for me. In that moment, I felt a release of shame and a heavy burden lifted from me. I told my secret to someone. The secret was out and no longer had power over me. I confessed with my mouth for the first time since then that I did something so unforgivable. And yet, God forgave me. This was not something that took Him by surprise. None the stupid things I did in my life up to that point compared to the one act of abortion. I could not change what I did, but I could learn to live again. Living dead was no longer an option for me. That night, I went home and started reading my bible and wept. It was a deep inconsolable weeping that I never experienced before. I was standing before the throne of God in my shame begging for forgiveness. I could not let this stand in the way of my relationship with God. I had to do something about it. I grieved the loss of the baby for a little while and slowly accepted forgiveness for what I did. Then came a hope. A hope that one day I would see that baby. For now, I chose to help others that found themselves in the position of making that very hard decision.

Dawn took her time with me to teach me and show me what being a Christian was all about. Even though I had been involved with church, I had no idea what a Christian did. Early on, my mentor, Mr. Willis, showed me those things; however, I was never ready to fully commit my life, so I confessed and half-listened. The seeds were planted by plenty of God-fearing people. I believed God sent Dawn into my life to help me really understand. I liked to say that I was through with needing to be perfect, but sometimes, the need for perfection still rose up inside me. I found that in perfection there was disappointment because life was messy sometimes. I knew I had messy parts to my life, but I also knew that I know that Jesus Christ would not leave me that way. Each new day was a new opportunity to know my Savior more and more. The more I got to know Jesus, the more I realized that He did not expect perfection from me. He only wanted my love and devotion to Him and to serve others out of nothing other than love. In the previous chapter, I said I had no idea what true love was. I did not have it all figured out, but I did know that love was an action word. The Bible laid out the characteristics of love in 1 Corinthians 13 saying "Love is patient and kind; love does not envy or boast; it is not arrogant or rude. It does not insist on its own way; it is not irritable or resentful; it does not rejoice at wrongdoing, but rejoices with the truth. Love bears all things, believes all things, hopes all things, endures all things" (1 Corinthians 13: 4-7, ESV). This kind of love was not natural for me; however, with God, I could love like this. It was possible.

Dawn showed me this kind of love when she came into my life. At that time in my life, I was nowhere near loving like God showed me. I was doing everything opposite, and I decided to get real with God because of love. I wanted to be loved and accepted. But by who? My friends, families, and social groups. Yes, those people too, but ultimately to understand real love was to get the truth from God. As a Christian in this era of time, I needed to reach others through love. Condemning someone for their sins was not going to lead them to

repentance; instead it would shut them out and isolate them further. If that happened, then how effective
would you be for the kingdom?

You see, Dawn demonstrated real love by not judg-
ing me but instead by going to the Word of God. Oh,
how I laugh now, but at the time, it was not funny. I
thought deep thought about whatever issue I was fac-
ing. I obsessed about the issue, and then I would go to
Dawn's house and ask her. She would quote scripture to
me like there was no tomorrow. She was able to do that
with me because I wanted to know what God said about
it. She held me up with love, prayer, and scripture until
I could do it for myself. She had no idea what she was
getting herself into when she met me. We became such
good friends because of what God did through her.

Dawn and I each had a son about the same age. They
became friends first. Jimmy and Jordan were like two
peas in a pod. Where one was the other was sure to follow. When Jimmy died from a drug overdose, it was
Dawn and her family that held me up when I could not
stand. It was a real test of my faith during that time.
Nothing made sense to me. I only knew my boy was
gone. My heart was so broken into pieces, but so were
their lives. Jimmy had become a part of Dawn's family
that losing him was like losing one of her family members. It was love that got us through that. After some
time of mourning, Dawn felt led to start an addiction

support group at our church. She asked me if I wanted to be involved, and I jumped at the opportunity to help others with their addictions. I needed to do something. We spent even more time together. I was learning ministry from her. She took the scary out of it for me. I did not know what to expect, but instead of a scary experience, it was rewarding to see people coming alive again. It made me feel better to see people kicking the devil in his teeth and overcoming his scheme to destroy.

Fresh Hope

I was empowered by a feeling of making the devil pay for everything he did to me or convinced me to do to myself and a feeling of seeing people set free from lies. Because of this empowerment, I started sharing my faith to anyone who would listen. I got free and wanted everyone else free too. I longed to step on the battlefield and become a soldier for Christ. I did not know where to begin. I did not realize the cost either. I learned over the years that a person must first live the lesson before it can ever be taught to anyone else. Sometimes, God allowed me to go through difficulties to grow me and prepare me for the battlefield. My battlefield happened to be in mental health. I struggled for so long that I thought I was always going to be broken, and by association, my family would be broken too. That was not the plan God had for me; instead, He opened my heart and my spiritual eyes to see this challenge as a lesson in life of overcoming my struggles through His power, love, and wisdom.

I thought about starting a support group for those with mental health challenges. I started searching for similar groups and found Fresh Hope for Mental Health. I considered this organization because it would bring faith into my recovery and help me to maintain my wellness. I did not have to give up on the Bible like some wanted me to do. I read so much that the lines of reality and supernatural collided together. They collided so much that when I became manic, due to not being medicated, I believed I was Jesus. Those who told me not to read the Bible anymore only meant well, but it was the worst thing I could do. I knew in my heart that God was going to heal me and soaking in His Word was going to be key for me. People just did not want to see me getting sick and quoting scripture to everyone because, at the time, I called everyone out on their misdeeds and shortcomings. But I could not give up my faith to be well; instead, I needed my faith to be well. I liked Fresh Hope because the pastor, Brad, brought the mental health part and the Word of God together in a way that was healing and empowering. It was a lot of hard work, but the reward was so worth the price of being uncomfortable in the process. God chose to heal me through medicine, and I am okay with that.

I sent a link for Fresh Hope to Pastor Tony to ask his opinion. He took a look at it and replied that there were no New Jersey meetings. He asked me to sign up for the newsletter and gather more information. At the time, I was oblivious to starting a meeting myself. After some time of careful consideration and prayer, I decided I wanted to start a Fresh Hope group in New Jersey. I got the information for training and enrolled in the Fresh Hope facilitator training with the recommendation from my pastor. After months of training and planning, our first Fresh Hope meeting started in February of 2020. We were learning and growing together in our similar, yet different, journeys. I hoped more churches would host Fresh Hope meetings all across New Jersey. The need is great.

I found my purpose. In facilitating the group meetings, I have learned to accept my diagnosis and, most importantly, live well in spite of it. I am so much more than bipolar disorder. I am a wife, a mother, a sister, a friend. I am an author, a really good cook, among so many other things. I am discovering a whole new level of myself that I never knew existed. Romans says, "And we know that all things work together for good to them that love God, to them who are called according to His purpose" (Romans 8:28, NIV). God knew everything I was going to go through, and not once did He ever give up on me. In fact, He already had a plan. He was using it all for good. I hope that by reading my story you will be empowered to fight your own good fight. If you or someone you know would like more information on

Fresh Hope for Mental Health, you can find more information on the website at www.freshhope.us

I have gained a new appreciation for my weaknesses. The more the enemy points out my weaknesses the more I lift up the name of Jesus Christ. I trust that no matter what I go through, I am not alone. Jesus is with me. I know that He will work all things out for my good.

I have been healed through Jesus Christ and medications. This is where my faith meets my life. I have faith and assured hope that I will not remain this way. On that great and glorious day, I will have a new body and mind. There will one day be no more sickness. I am learning how to live well in this moment and present condition through my relationship with Jesus Christ.

I want to give Jesus Christ all the glory and honor for this healing. Isaiah 53:5 "But he was wounded for our transgressions, he was bruised for our iniquities: the chastisement of our peace was upon him; and with his stripes we are healed". I may still have some symptoms that I am challenged with, but the real victory is that it no longer holds me captive in self-doubt and shame. In fact, having Jesus in my life has empowered to not shrink back in fear but to boldly rise up and fight the good fight.

I encourage you to put your trust and confidence in Jesus Christ. He alone can save you, heal you and create in you a new heart. It is as simple as believing that He is the Son of God who came to this earth to die for you. And that he also in three days rose from the dead. If you have never asked Jesus into your heart or maybe you have asked Jesus into your heart but you want to renew your relationship with him, you can do it right now where you are by humbling yourself and repeating this prayer:

Dear Jesus, I know that I am a sinner, in need of a savior. I choose today to make you the Lord and Savior of my life. I ask you Jesus to come into my life and change me. Thank you, Lord, for the free gift of salvation. In Jesus name I pray. Amen.

Now I encourage you to find a bible believing church where you can grow, learn and fellowship with other believers such as yourself.

CPSIA information can be obtained
at www.ICGtesting.com
Printed in the USA
LVHW051434171120
671903LV00008B/545